YUMA COUNTY LIBRARY DISTRICT

D0600708

D. Yuma, AZ 85364
(928) 782-1871
www.yumalibrary.org

DISCARDED BY
YUMA COUNTY
LIBRARY DISTRICT

A **TRUE** BOOK™

DIY
DO IT YOURSELF

Amazing Makerspace
Basic Machines

KRISTINA A. HOLZWEISS

Children's Press®
An Imprint of Scholastic Inc.

Content Consultant
Shaunna Smith, EdD
Assistant Professor of Educational Technology
Department of Curriculum
Texas State University, San Marcos, Texas

Library of Congress Cataloging-in-Publication Data
Names: Holzweiss, Kristina A., author.
Title: Amazing makerspace DIY basic machines / by Kristina Holzweiss.
Other titles: True book.
Description: New York : Children's Press/Scholastic, [2017] | Series: A true book
Identifiers: LCCN 2016058679 | ISBN 9780531238448 (library binding) | ISBN 9780531240953 (pbk.)
Subjects: LCSH: Machinery—Juvenile literature. | Robots—Juvenile literature. | Makerspaces—
    Juvenile literature. | Handicraft—Juvenile literature.
Classification: LCC TJ147 .H645 2017 | DDC 621.8/1—dc23
LC record available at https://lccn.loc.gov/2016058679

No part of this publication may be reproduced in whole or in part, or stored in a retrieval system,
or transmitted in any form or by any means, electronic, mechanical, photocopying, recording, or
otherwise, without written permission of the publisher. For information regarding permission,
write to Scholastic Inc., Attention: Permissions Department, 557 Broadway, New York, NY 10012.
© 2018 Scholastic Inc.

All rights reserved. Published in 2018 by Children's Press, an imprint of Scholastic Inc.
Printed in China 62

SCHOLASTIC, CHILDREN'S PRESS, A TRUE BOOK™, and associated logos are trademarks and/or
registered trademarks of Scholastic Inc., 557 Broadway, New York, NY 10012.
1 2 3 4 5 6 7 8 9 10 R 27 26 25 24 23 22 21 20 19 18

Front cover: Brush Bot project
Back cover: Student with Automaton project

Find the Truth!

Everything you are about to read is true *except* for one of the sentences on this page.

Which one is **TRUE**?

T or F Robots can help save lives.

T or F Gravity is a type of force produced only by Earth.

Find the answers in this book.

Contents

THE **BIG** TRUTH!

Robot Helpers

Automaton

4

Ramp walker

3 Automaton

How can you combine simple machines
to do something more complex?

Famous Inventors and Pioneers

Timeline

Warning!
Some of these projects use pointy,
sticky, hot, or otherwise risky objects.
Keep a trusted adult around to
help you out and keep you safe.

You Can Be a Maker!

Makers are always thinking about problems and searching for ways to solve them. They create machines and test them out. Then they think about what they learned and improve their work until it is perfect.

You can be a maker, too! This book will help you create basic machines. Read through all the directions of a project first, then follow along to make the machine in your **makerspace**. Then experiment with your creations to make them even better!

Automaton

Ramp Walker

Brush Bot

Think Ahead!

How do you think this machine moves when it walks?

CHAPTER 1

Ramp Walker

In this project, you will build a two-legged robot. This robot can walk on its own, but it doesn't have a motor or any electronic parts. All you'll need to build it on your makerspace table are some common craft supplies. How is this possible? It's simple! The force of **gravity** will power your creation.

Wooden walking toys were popular in the early 1900s.

Gravity

Gravity is a force of attraction between objects. Every object in the universe has a certain amount of gravity. The larger an object is, the stronger its gravitational, or gravity-related, pull. For example, the sun's gravity is strong enough to keep planets in **orbit** around it. Earth's gravity keeps people, buildings, and other objects from floating off into space.

The sun's gravity keeps planets, asteroids, comets, and other objects in orbit.

Skateboarders sometimes use inclined planes to gain the speed they need to do fancy tricks.

Inclined Plane

To get your robot moving, you'll need a ramp for it to walk down. A ramp is a type of **simple machine** called an inclined plane. It can use the pull of gravity to move an object downward. But instead of gravity pulling it straight down to the ground, the object is pulled downward across the length of the ramp.

11

Build a Ramp Walker

What You Need

- ☐ Scissors
- ☐ Cardboard
- ☐ Sharp pencil
- ☐ 1 small sheet of felt
- ☐ Glue
- ☐ Ruler
- ☐ Thin wooden skewer, 10 to 15 inches (25 to 38 centimeters) long
- ☐ 3 wooden beads at least 1 inch (2.5 cm) wide, with the same shape and size
- ☐ Small, thin rubber bands
- ☐ 2 craft sticks
- ☐ Masking tape

Project Instructions

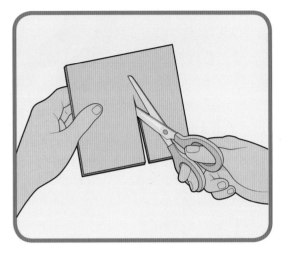

1. Using scissors, cut two strips 3 inches (7.6 cm) long and 1.5 inches (3.8 cm) wide from the cardboard. These are the walker's legs.

Be careful not to poke yourself
when creating these holes.

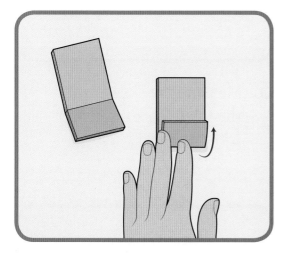

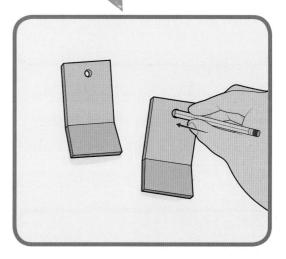

2. Fold each cardboard leg about 1 inch (2.5 cm) from the bottom. This creates a "foot" that rests flat on the table.

3. With the pencil tip, poke a hole in each leg centered about 0.5 inch (1.3 cm) from the top.

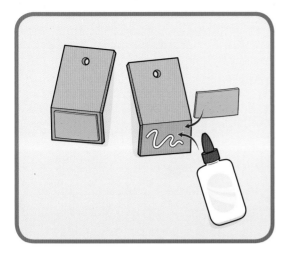

4. Cut out two pieces of felt the same size and shape as the feet. Glue a piece to the bottom of each foot.

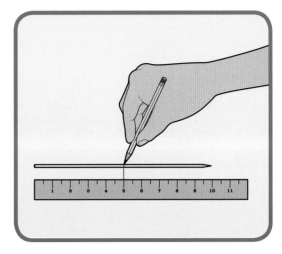

5. Measure the skewer with the ruler. Mark the center with the pencil.

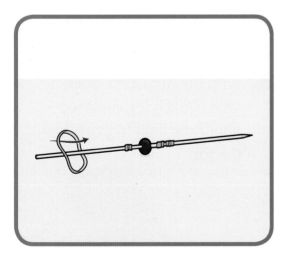

6. Slide a wooden bead onto the skewer's center. If it is loose, wrap rubber bands around the skewer on each side of the bead to keep it in place.

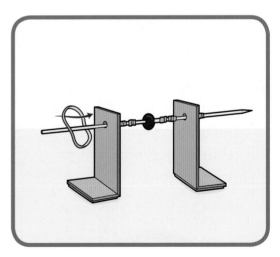

7. Add a leg on each side of the skewer as shown. Leave a little space between the legs and the bead.

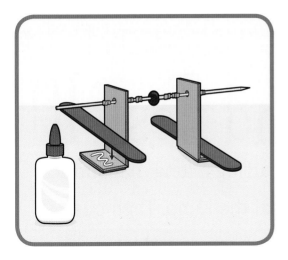

8. Glue a craft stick flat on top of each foot so it is centered on the foot and rests against the leg.

9. Slide a wooden bead onto each end of the skewer.

The felt on the bottom of the walker's feet helps keep it from slipping.

Move It and Test It!

Make a ramp for your walker using a long, flat surface. Place your walker at the top of the ramp. Then push gently down on one end of the skewer and let go to make it walk. The walker should sway from side to side as it moves. Depending on what you use to build your ramp, the walker might slide around and have trouble gripping the surface. If this happens, add strips of masking tape for it to walk on.

Change It!

Your walker might move differently if you make a few changes to its design. Try some of these ideas. Test the results. What differences do you notice? Why do you think they occur?

- Design a walker with four legs instead of two.
- Build a walker with shorter or longer legs.
- Make a steeper ramp.

Think Ahead!

**How does energy
move from the battery
to the motor?**

Brush Bot

Your first machine relied on the natural force of Earth's gravity to keep it in motion. Now you will take your making to the next level. This time, you will build a machine with its own power source: a small motor and battery pack. This creation will not need a ramp. It will be able to walk on its own across a variety of surfaces!

The first electric motors strong enough to accomplish tasks were developed in the 1830s.

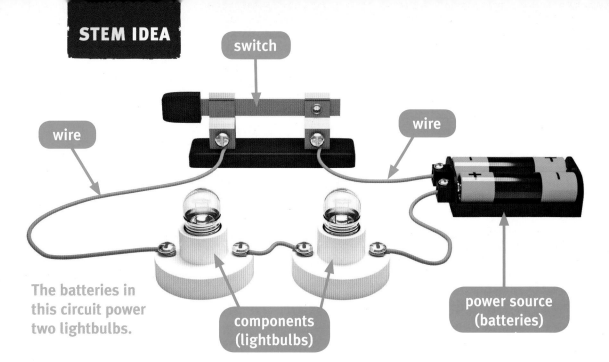

switch

wire

wire

The batteries in this circuit power two lightbulbs.

components (lightbulbs)

power source (batteries)

Electricity and Circuits

To build this robot, you will need to create an electrical **circuit**. A circuit is a looped path for electricity to follow. The electricity starts at a power source such as a battery. Then it travels along wires to the object it is powering. For your robot, this object is a motor. The motor will use the electricity to move the short shaft that sticks out of it, which will move the robot. Then to complete the circuit's loop, the electricity continues along the path back to the battery.

Positive and Negative

As you build your circuit, carefully note the positive and negative ends of batteries and wires. This will help you make sure electricity flows in the correct direction. The chart below details how wires and each end of a battery are marked.

Charge	Symbol on Battery	Wire Color
Positive	+	Red
Negative	−	Black

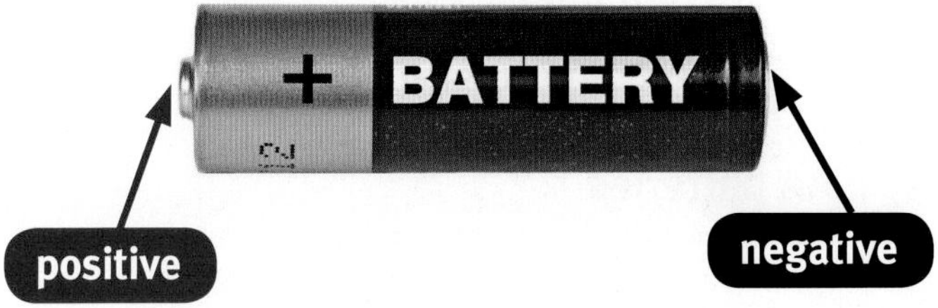

+ BATTERY

positive

negative

All batteries have a positive and negative part.

Build a Brush Bot

What You Need

- Battery holder for 2 AA batteries
- Wire stripper
- 3-volt DC motor
- Cork
- Scrub brush
- Hot glue gun
- Electrical tape
- Duct tape
- Construction paper, ribbons, markers, and other decorations
- 2 AA batteries

Project Instructions

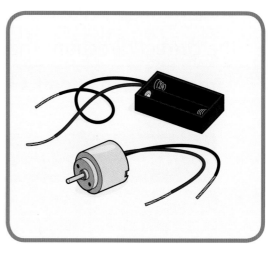

1. Make sure the battery holder is switched off. Use the wire stripper to strip about 1 inch (2.5 cm) of coating off the ends of the wires on the battery holder and the motor.

Billions of batteries are
sold in the United States
each year.

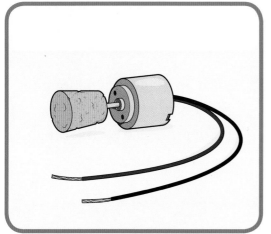

2. Press the cork onto the motor's shaft (the small rod that sticks out). The shaft should go into the bottom of the cork.

3. Set the motor on one end of the back of the scrub brush so the cork hangs off the edge.

4. Place the battery holder at the other end of the brush. Make sure the battery holder's red and black wires can reach the motor's red and black wires.

5. With an adult's help, hot glue the motor and the battery holder in place on the brush.

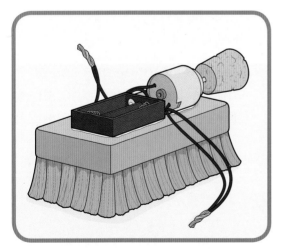

6. Twist the stripped ends of the motor's red wire and the battery holder's red wire together tightly. Do the same with the black wires.

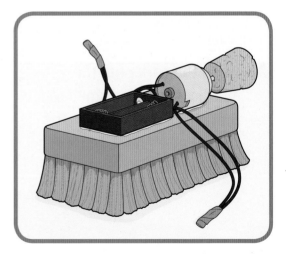

7. Wrap the connected wires with electrical tape.

8. If you want to, secure the wires to the brush with duct tape so they don't hang off the sides.

9. Decorate the brush bot with your construction paper or other supplies!

Make sure you attach the wires and insert the batteries correctly. Otherwise, your bot won't move.

Move It and Test It!

Find a flat, wide-open surface, such as a table or the floor, where your bot will have plenty of space to move. Insert the two AA batteries into the bot's battery case. Make sure the positive and negative ends of the batteries line up with the positive and negative symbols in the battery case. Once the batteries are in, flip on the power switch. The cork adds weight to the motor's shaft, causing the whole brush to vibrate and move your bot around.

Change It!

Make your brush bot change course by altering the way you put it together. Try the variations below and see what happens. What differences do you notice? What do you think causes the changes?

- Take off the cork.
- Attach the cork so it is off-center on the motor's shaft.
- Use a different size brush.
- Place the brush bot on the ramp you used for the ramp walker.

Robot Helpers

So far, we've built two robots that can move around on their own. However, today's most amazing robots can do a lot more. They can accomplish all kinds of incredible things. Examples range from exploring hard-to-reach places to performing complicated tasks.

Exploring Distant Worlds

Robots are very helpful for exploring places that humans can't reach. NASA (National Aeronautics and Space Administration) scientists have sent robots called rovers to the surface of Mars. The robots take photos and collect other data about the planet. Then they send them back to Earth for study.

Under the Sea

Robots can also help explore extreme ocean depths. Like rovers on Mars, they collect samples and take a variety of measurements of their surroundings. They also often have video cameras so scientists on the surface can see what the robots see.

Robot Doctors

Believe it or not, robots can help save people's lives. Surgeons sometimes use robots to complete difficult procedures. A surgical robot can perform small, precise movements that are very hard for humans to do. In some cases, these robots can be controlled remotely. This means doctors can use the technology to perform surgeries from anywhere in the world.

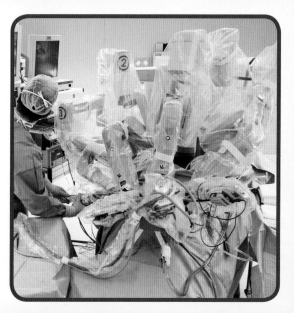

Think Ahead!

Which parts of this machine do you think are the gears?

Automaton

Some of the earliest robots ever created were devices called automatons. These machines used a combination of gears, levers, and other simple machines to move in entertaining ways. One famous automaton was a **humanoid** figure that could write with a pen. Another looked like a band and played music. In this project, you'll use some common craft items to build your own colorful automaton.

The earliest automatons were built thousands of years ago in ancient Greece.

Complex Machines

In this project, you'll combine several basic parts into a **complex machine**. As each piece in the automaton moves, it causes other pieces to move as well. This causes a chain reaction of movement, so when you turn the handle on the automaton, all the other pieces come to life.

This automaton, built in Japan in about 1860, features an archer that can pick up and fire arrows.

A bicycle's gears transfer movement from the pedals to a wheel.

Gears

To build an automaton, you will first need some gears. These are circular pieces that connect and spin around. As they spin, they make connected gears spin, too. Gears are found in many machines. For example, you can see them inside clocks and watches, in car engines, and on bicycles. The gears in your automaton will make a creature move up and down.

Build an Automaton

- ○ **Small cardboard box; its width must be shorter than the length of your skewers**
- ○ **Scissors**
- ○ **Duct tape**
- ○ **Pencil**
- ○ **Drinking straw**
- ○ **Glue**
- ○ **Thick foam sheet**
- ○ **Ruler**
- ○ **2 wooden skewers**
- ○ **Craft supplies for decorating, such as pom-poms, markers, crayons, colored pencils, googly eyes, and glitter**

Project Instructions

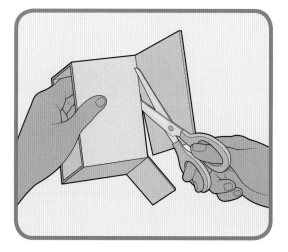

1. Cut the flaps off the cardboard box with scissors.

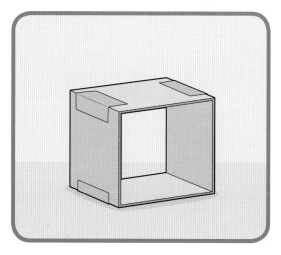

2. Place the box on its side. This is the frame of the automaton. Add duct tape across each corner of the frame to **reinforce** it.

3. Use the pencil to poke a hole through the top of the frame.

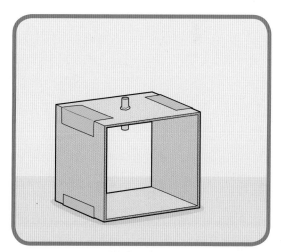

4. Cut a piece of straw about 1.5 inches (3.8 cm) long. Put this piece into the hole and glue it in place. Set it aside to dry.

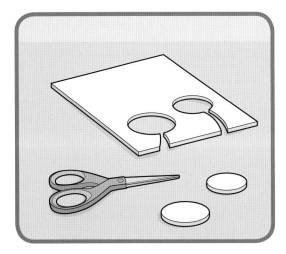

5. Cut out two foam circles, one 2.5 inches (6 cm) and one 3 inches (7.6 cm) in **diameter**. Both should fit in the box.

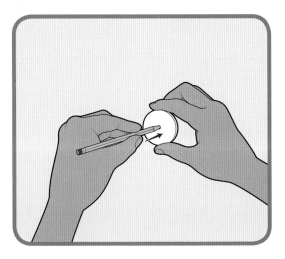

6. Poke a small, off-center hole in the smaller gear with the tip of a pencil or a skewer.

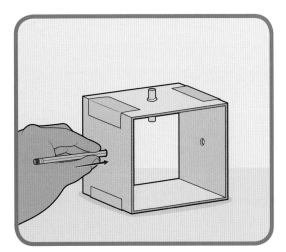

7. Poke holes in both sides of your frame 2 inches (5 cm) from the top.

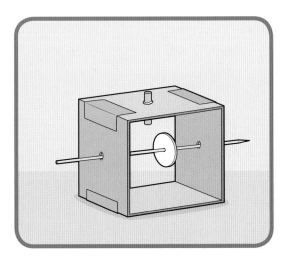

8. Push a skewer through one hole in the frame, through the hole in the smaller gear, and then through the hole on the opposite side of the frame.

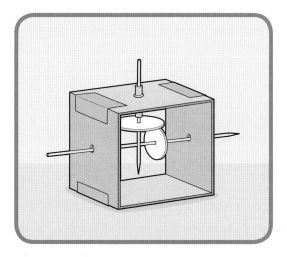

9. Push the other skewer through the straw in the frame's top through the center of the larger gear, so the circle rests on the small gear.

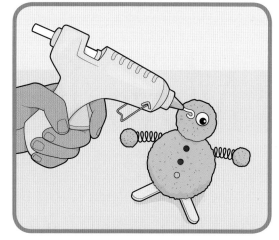

10. Create an object or creature for the automaton with craft supplies that are not too heavy.

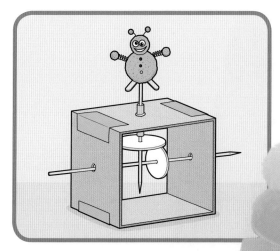

11. Glue the creation to the top skewer.

No matter what side of the large gear your small gear is on, your automaton will work.

Move It and Test It!

Once all the glue is dry, turn the handle to make your object or creature jump up and down. Adjust the smaller foam circle underneath the larger one, and test it out by turning the handle until you find a motion that you like. When you are ready, glue the smaller circle to its horizontal skewer so it stays in place. ★

Change It!

You can change the movement of your creature by adjusting the automaton's circular gears. Try the ideas below. What differences do you notice? Why do you think they occur?

- Add another circle to the horizontal skewer.
- Change the position of the hole on the smaller circle.
- Change the position of the hole on the larger circle.

Famous Inventors and Pioneers

Ada Lovelace

(1815–1852) was a mathematician who created the first program for Charles Babbage's computer. As a result, she is often considered history's first computer programmer.

Charles Babbage

(1791–1871) was an inventor and mathematician best known for designing the world's first computer. Though Babbage's design was revolutionary, he never actually finished building a working version. He was still working on it when he died. Other scientists completed his work after his death.

Karel Capek

(1890–1938) was a novelist and playwright whose works often dealt with technology and science. In 1920, Capek wrote a play about human-like machines. He called them robots, and the name stuck.

George Devol

(1912–2011) invented the world's first programmable robotic arm. This

device, called the Unimate, allowed companies to manufacture cars and other items faster and more cheaply than ever before.

Joseph Engelberger

(1925–2015) was an engineer and inventor who founded the world's first robotics company. As a result, he is known as the father of robotics. Engelberger's creations were used to improve manufacturing practices and medical techniques.

Theo Jansen

(1948–) is an artist whose work takes the exploration of movement to new heights. An ongoing project is a set of self-propelled "Strandbeests." Each of these sculptures combines many simple machines into a complex one that can walk, on its own, along the beach.

Timeline

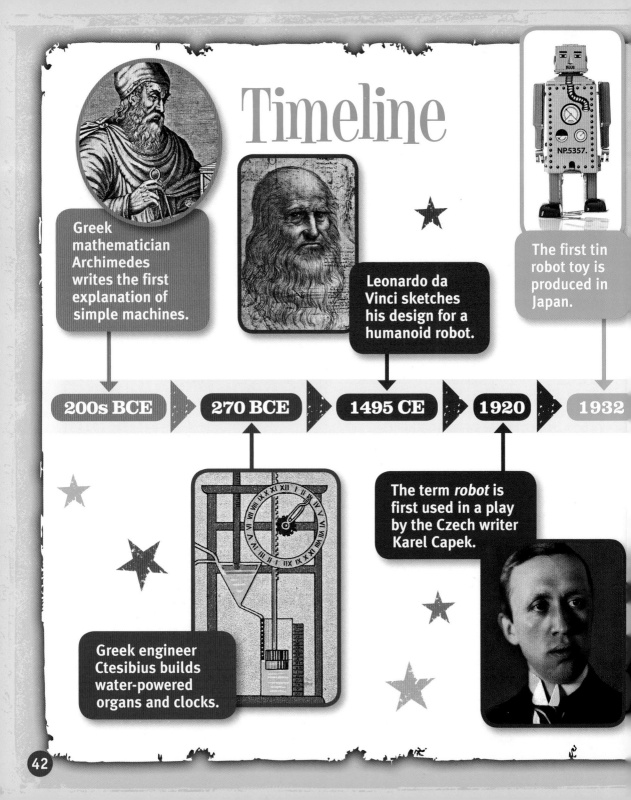

Greek mathematician Archimedes writes the first explanation of simple machines.

Leonardo da Vinci sketches his design for a humanoid robot.

The first tin robot toy is produced in Japan.

200s BCE ▶ **270 BCE** ▶ **1495 CE** ▶ **1920** ▶ **1932**

The term *robot* is first used in a play by the Czech writer Karel Capek.

Greek engineer Ctesibius builds water-powered organs and clocks.

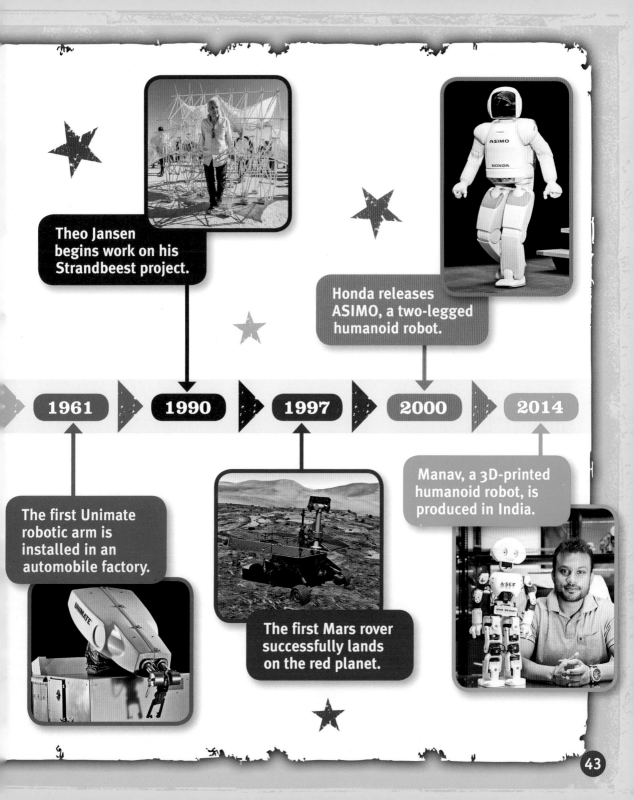

Theo Jansen begins work on his Strandbeest project.

Honda releases ASIMO, a two-legged humanoid robot.

1961

1990

1997

2000

2014

The first Unimate robotic arm is installed in an automobile factory.

The first Mars rover successfully lands on the red planet.

Manav, a 3D-printed humanoid robot, is produced in India.

True Statistics

Number of robotic surgeries performed each year in the United States: More than 400,000

Number of rovers that have successfully traveled to the surface of Mars: 4

Number of Mars rovers that are still active: 2

Depth reached by the robotic submarine *Nereus* in 2009: 6.8 mi. (11 km)

Weight of the original Unimate robotic arm: 4,000 lb. (1,814 kg)

Number of new industrial robots sold in 2015: 253,748

NP.5357.

Did you find the truth?

(T) Robots can help save lives.

(F) Gravity is a type of force produced only by Earth.

Resources

Books

Doudna, Kelly. *The Kids' Book of Simple Machines: Cool Projects & Activities That Make Science Fun!* Minneapolis: Mighty Media Kids, 2015.

Gray, Susan Heinrichs. *Experiments With Electricity*. New York: Children's Press, 2012.

Gray, Susan Heinrichs. *Experiments With Motion*. New York: Children's Press, 2012.

Wilkinson, Karen, and Mike Petrich. *The Art of Tinkering: Meet 150+ Makers Working at the Intersection of Art, Science & Technology*. San Francisco: Weldon Owen, 2013.

Visit this Scholastic website for more information on basic machines:

★ www.factsfornow.scholastic.com
Enter the keywords **Basic Machines**

Important Words

circuit (SUR-kit) a complete, looped path for an electrical current

complex machine (kuhm-PLEKS muh-SHEEN) a device that combines multiple simple machines into one working unit

diameter (dye-AM-uh-tur) the length of a straight line through the center of a circle, connecting opposite sides

gravity (GRAV-ih-tee) the force that pulls things toward the center of an object

humanoid (HYOO-muh-noyd) in the shape of a human being

makerspace (MAY-kur-spays) any place where people plan, design, tinker, create, change, and fix things for fun or to solve problems

orbit (OR-bit) the curved path followed by a moon, planet, or satellite as it circles a planet or the sun

reinforce (ree-in-FORS) to make something stronger or more effective

simple machine (SIM-puhl muh-SHEEN) a basic mechanical device for applying force

Index

Page numbers in **bold** indicate illustrations.

About the Author

Kristina A. Holzweiss was selected by *School Library Journal* as the School Librarian of the Year in 2015. She is the founder of SLIME—Students of Long Island Maker Expo—and the president of Long Island LEADS, a nonprofit organization to promote STEAM education and the maker movement. In her free time, Kristina enjoys making memories with her husband, Mike, and their three children, Tyler, Riley, and Lexy.

Scholastic Library Publishing wants to especially thank Kristina A. Holzweiss, Bay Shore Middle School, and all the kids who worked as models in these books for their time and generosity.

PHOTOGRAPHS ©: 3: Javier Larrea/age fotostock; 4 markers and throughout: photosync/Shutterstock; 5 colored papers and throughout: MNI/Shutterstock; 10: BSIP SA/Alamy Images; 11: Izf/Dreamstime; 12 rubber bands and throughout: studiof22byricardorocha/iStockphoto; 12 graph paper and throughout: billnoll/iStockphoto; 13 bottom right: photastic/Shutterstock; 20: haryigit/Thinkstock; 21 left: All For You/Shutterstock; 21 battery and throughout: Kotkot32/Shutterstock; 22 bottom left: Nik Merkulov/Shutterstock; 28: JPL-Caltech/MSSS/NASA; 29 top: Teddy Seguin; 29 bottom: Javier Larrea/age fotostock; 32: Adam Hart-Davis/Science Sourceights Managed; 33: Oleksiy Maksymenko/age fotostock; 34 top left: Aksenova Natalya/Shutterstock; 34 top right: GooDween123/Shutterstock; 34 bottom: 2Frogs Studio/Shutterstock; 39 center: Marsel307/Dreamstime; 39 right: Voronina Svetlana/Shutterstock; 39 left: microstocker/iStockphoto; 40 left: Science and Society/Superstock, Inc.; 40 right: Pictorial Press Ltd./Alamy Images; 41 top left: Popperfoto/Getty Images; 41 top right: From the Collections of The Henry Ford; 41 bottom left: Peter Menzel/Science Source; 41 bottom right: ZUMA Press/Alamy Images; 42 top left: North Wind Picture Archives/Alamy Images; 42 top center: Photo Researchers/Getty Images; 42 top right: urbanbuzz/Alamy Images; 42 bottom left: Mary Evans Picture Library/Alamy Images; 42 bottom right: Popperfoto/Getty Images; 43 top right: catwalker/Shutterstock; 43 bottom left: Science & Society Picture Library/Getty Images; 43 bottom center: Stocktrek Images/Thinkstock; 43 bottom right: Jasonprost/Wikimedia; 43 top left: ZUMA Press/Alamy Images; 44: urbanbuzz/Alamy Images.

All instructional illustrations by Brown Bird Design.
All other images by Bianca Alexis Photography.